THE ADVENTURES OF MOLLY BLUE

MOLLY'S BIRTHDAY PARTY

By A. H. DeVito and Kimberly Blevins

Illustrations by Jeanette Baker

DEDICATION
To the adoptive and foster families,
and to all those who make a safe place
that kids call home.

ISBN: X1499168985
ISBN 13: 9781499168983
Library of Congress Control Number: 2014907385
CreateSpace Independent Publishing Platform, North Charleston, SC

Visit us at www.MollyBlue.net
Email the authors at ThunderBlab@ymail.com
Find us on Facebook at
www.Facebook.com/SuperNose

Molly Blue is a lovable Labrador retriever with a special gift - her super nose. Molly lives with her master, Skyler Blue, and his little brother, Reed. Together with the boys Molly enjoys life and learns many important lessons.

The Blue family planned a big party to say,
"Happy Birthday" to Molly on her special day!!

Don and Kaye brought their dog, Lucky.
April and David arrived with Chucky.

Molly's friend, Bella, arrived with Michelle.
The puppies Dante and Lucy were there as well.

The kids sang for Molly a 'Happy Birthday' song,
and the puppies did their best to try to sing along.

Mom surprised the kids with toys in gift packs.
Molly ate birthday cake made from puppy snacks.

Molly's friends played pin the tail on the cat.

The little dog, Tobey, he was the best at that.

The girls had fun painting flowers on their faces...

...while the boys were having slot car races.

Then a question came from Skyler's friend, Jerome,
"Can you tell us how Molly came to your home?"

Skyler said, "We got Molly when I turned four.
We first met her at the puppy pet store.
And when I saw Molly I knew for sure,
I said, she's the one – I'll take her!"

The man warned, "Oh that one, she's a handful indeed.
She eats like a horse and she's growing like a weed."

"And can I tell you about those sharp puppy teeth?
She chewed through her crate, on top and underneath!"

But I said, "I'm not worried about that, by golly.
I'm taking her with me, I'm naming her Molly."

"We learned about her super nose right away,
she found my lost toys that very same day."

"Ever since Molly joined the Blue family,
not a day has gone by without smiles and glee."

Just then Skyler's friend, Jessica, started to cry.
She turned to Skyler wiping a tear from her eye,
"I wish I had family like you and your brother,
I live alone with just me and my mother."

Skyler thought about it for a minute or two,
then replied, "I think I know what is bothering you."

"Now, family isn't just parents, sisters or brothers.
What's important is the love you have for each other."

"One boy lives just with his mom, his name is Jason."

"Another boy lives with his dad, his name is Grayson."

"Some kids stay with grandparents, an uncle or aunt.
Many foster parents help when a kid's parents can't."

"Not all families are made of one mom and one dad.
And if yours is not, that doesn't have to be bad.
In our home it's just Mom, my brother Reed and me.
With plenty of love we are a happy family."

Jessica smiled and said, "You know, Skyler, you are right.
Mom kisses my cheek each day, tucks me in bed each night."

"When we compare ourselves to other people, I guess,
we will always see some with more and some with less."

Reed said, "Jessica, I'll tell you how to be happy for a fact -
be thankful for what you have, don't think
about what you lack."

Tim added, "We should be thankful for what we've got, whether we have little or whether we have a lot."

The kids thought about it and all would agree,
they were each lucky to be part of a loving family.

The kids knew they were blessed as they went out to play,
with Molly and her friends on this special birthday.

THE END

LESSON QUESTIONS:

1) What day is Molly's birthday?

2) What game were the dogs playing
   in the yard? Who won?

3) How old was Skyler when Molly came to
   live with the Blues?

4) What did Skyler learn about Molly on the first day?

5) Why do you think Jessica was sad?

BONUS:

Can you find the cupcakes in the scenes throughout the story?

Find them before Earl the Squirrel steals them!

The kids learned that love is one of the most important things for families to share.

Enhance your learning by checking out the following:

ASPCA Adoption	U.S. Dept. HHS – children's bureau	Anti-bullying programs
www.aspca.org/adopt	www.acf.hhs.gov/programs/cb	www.stopbullying.gov